The Constitution of the
State of Tennessee:
A Quick Reference Guide

Bootblack Budget Books
Copyright 2018 ©
ISBN-13: 978-1722921200
ISBN-10: 172292120X

Contents:

PREAMBLE:

Whereas, The people of the territory of the United States south of the river Ohio, having the right of admission into the General Government as a member State thereof, consistent with the Constitution of the United States, and the act of Cession of the State of North Carolina, recognizing the ordinance for the government of the territory of the United States north west of the Ohio River, by their Delegates and Representatives in Convention assembled, did on the sixth day of February, in the year of our Lord one thousand seven hundred and ninety-six, ordain and establish a Constitution, or form of government, and mutually agreed with each other to form themselves into a free and independent State by the name of the State of Tennessee, and,

Whereas, The General Assembly of the said State of Tennessee, (pursuant to the third section of the tenth article of the Constitution,) by an act passed on the Twenty-seventh day of November, in the year of our Lord one thousand eight hundred and thirty-three, entitled, "An Act" to provide for the calling of a Convention, passed in obedience to the declared will of the voters of the State, as expressed at the general election of August, in the year of our Lord one thousand eight hundred and thirty-three, did authorize and provide for the election by the people of delegates and representatives, to meet at Nashville, in Davidson County, on the third Monday in May, in the year of our Lord one thousand eight hundred and thirty-four, for the purpose of revising and amending, or changing, the Constitution, and said Convention did accordingly meet and form a Constitution, which was submitted to the people, and was ratified by them, on the first Friday in March, in the year of our Lord one thousand eight hundred and thirty-five; and,

Whereas, The General Assembly of said State of Tennessee, under and in virtue of the first section of the first article of the declaration of Rights, contained in and forming a part of the existing Constitution of the State, by an act passed on the fifteenth day of November, in the year of our Lord one thousand eight hundred and sixty-nine, did provide for the calling of a Convention by the people of the State, to meet at Nashville, on the second Monday in January, in the year of our Lord one thousand eight hundred and seventy, and for the election of delegates for the purpose of amending or revising the present Constitution, or forming and making a new Constitution; and,

Whereas, The people of the State, in the mode provided by said Act, have called said Convention, and elected Delegates to represent them therein; Now, therefore,

We, the Delegates and Representatives of the people of the State of Tennessee, duly elected, and in Convention assembled, in pursuance of said Act of Assembly, have ordained and established the following Constitution and form of government for this State, which we recommend to the people of Tennessee for their ratification: That is to say:

ARTICLE I: DECLARATION OF RIGHTS

Section 1. That all power is inherent in the people, and all free governments are founded on their authority, and instituted for their peace, safety, and happiness; for the advancement of those ends they have at all times, an unalienable and indefeasible right to alter, reform, or abolish the government in such manner as they may think proper.

Section 2. That government being instituted for the common benefit, the doctrine of non-resistance against arbitrary power and oppression is absurd, slavish, and destructive of the good and happiness of mankind.

Section 3. That all men have a natural and indefeasible right to worship Almighty God according to the dictates of their own conscience; that no man can of right be compelled to attend, erect, or support any place of worship, or to maintain any minister against his consent; that no human authority can, in any case whatever, control or interfere with the rights of conscience; and that no preference shall ever be given, by law, to any religious establishment or mode of worship.

Section 4. That no political or religious test, other than an oath to support the Constitution of the United States and of this State, shall ever be required as a qualification to any office or public trust under this state.

Section 5. That elections shall be free and equal, and the right of suffrage, as hereinafter declared, shall never be denied to any person entitled thereto, except upon a conviction by a jury of some infamous crime, previously ascertained and declared by law, and judgment thereon by court of competent jurisdiction.

Section 6. That the right of trial by jury shall remain inviolate, and no religious or political test shall ever be required as a qualification for jurors.

Section 7. That the people shall be secure in their persons, houses, papers and possessions, from unreasonable searches and seizures; and that general warrants, whereby an officer may be commanded to search suspected places, without evidence of the fact committed, or to seize any person or persons not named, whose offences are not particularly described and supported by evidence, are dangerous to liberty and ought not to be granted.

Section 8. That no man shall be taken or imprisoned, or disseized of his freehold, liberties or privileges, or outlawed, or exiled, or in any manner destroyed or deprived of his life, liberty or property, but by the judgment of his peers, or the law of the land.

Section 9. That in all criminal prosecutions, the accused hath the right to be heard by himself and his counsel; to demand the nature and cause of the accusation against him, and to have a copy thereof, to meet the witnesses face to face, to have compulsory process for obtaining witnesses in his favor, and in prosecutions by indictment or presentment, a speedy public trial, by an impartial jury of the County in which the crime shall have been committed, and shall not be compelled to give evidence against himself.

Section 10. That no person shall, for the same offence, be twice put in jeopardy of life or limb.

Section 11. That laws made for the punishment of acts committed previous to the existence of such laws, and by them only declared criminal, are contrary to the principles of a free Government; wherefore no Ex post facto law shall be made.

Section 12. That no conviction shall work corruption of blood or forfeiture of estate. The estate of such persons as shall destroy their own lives shall descend or vest as in case of natural death. If any person be killed by casualty, there shall be no forfeiture in consequence thereof.

Section 13. That no person arrested and confined in jail shall be treated with unnecessary rigor.

Section 14. That no person shall be put to answer any criminal charge but by presentment, indictment or impeachment.

Section 15. That all prisoners shall be available by sufficient sureties, unless for capital offences, when the proof is evident, or the presumption great. And the privilege of the writ of Habeas Corpus shall not be suspended, unless when in case of rebellion or invasion, the General Assembly shall declare the public safety requires it.

Section 16. That excessive bail shall not be required, nor excessive fines imposed, nor cruel and unusual punishments inflicted.

Section 17. That all courts shall be open; and every man, for an injury done him in his lands, goods, person or reputation, shall have remedy by due course of law, and right and justice administered without sale, denial, or delay. Suits may be brought against the State in such manner and in such courts as the Legislature may by law direct.

Section 18. The Legislature shall pass no law authorizing imprisonment for debt in civil cases.

Section 19. That the printing presses shall be free to every person to examine the proceedings of the Legislature; or of any branch or officer of the government, and no law shall ever be made to restrain the right thereof. The free communication of thoughts and opinions, is one of the invaluable rights of man and every citizen may freely speak, write, and print on any subject, being responsible for the abuse of that liberty. But in prosecutions for the publication of papers investigating the official conduct of officers, or men in public capacity, the truth thereof may be given in evidence; and in all indictments for libel, the jury shall have a right to determine the law and the facts, under the direction of the court, as in other criminal cases.

Section 20. That no retrospective law, or law impairing the obligations of contracts, shall be made.

Section 21. That no man's particular services shall be demanded, or property taken, or applied to public use, without the consent of his representatives, or without just compensation being made therefore.

Section 22. That perpetuities and monopolies are contrary to the genius of a free State, and shall not be allowed.

Section 23. That the citizens have a right, in a peaceable manner, to assemble together for their common good, to instruct their representatives, and to apply to those invested with the powers of go eminent for redress of grievances, or other proper purposes, by address or remonstrance.

Section 24. That the sure and certain defense of a free people, is a well regulated militia; and, as standing armies in time of peace are dangerous to freedom, they ought to be avoided as far as the circumstances and safety of the community will admit; and that in all cases the military shall be kept in strict subordination to the civil authority.

Section 25. That no citizen of this State, except such as are employed in the army of the United States, or militia in actual service, shall be subjected to punishment under the martial or military law. That martial law, in the sense of the unrestricted power of military officers, or others, to dispose of the persons, liberties or property of the citizen, is inconsistent with the principles of free government, and is not confined to any department of the government of this State.

Section 26. That the citizens of this State have a right to keep and to bear arms for their common defense; but the Legislature shall have power, by law, to regulate the wearing of arms with a view to prevent crime.

Section 27. That no soldier shall, in time of peace, be quartered in any house without the consent of the owner; nor in time of war, but in a manner prescribed by law.

Section 28. That no citizen of this State shall be compelled to bear arms, provided he will pay an equivalent, to be ascertained by law.

Section 29. That an equal participation in the free navigation of the Mississippi, is one of the inherent rights of the citizens of this State; it cannot, therefore, be conceded to any prince, potentate, power, person or persons whatever.

Section 30. That no hereditary emoluments, privileges, or honors, shall ever be granted or conferred in this State.

Section 31. That the limits and boundaries of this State be ascertained, it is declared they are as hereafter mentioned, that is to say: Beginning on the extreme height of the Stone Mountain, at the place where the line of Virginia intersects it, in latitude thirty-six degrees and thirty minutes north; running thence along the extreme height of the said mountain, to the place where Watauga river breaks through it; thence a direct course to the top of the Yellow Mountain, where Bright's road crosses the same; thence along the ridge of said mountain, between the waters of Doe river and the waters of Rock creek, to the place where the road crosses the Iron Mountain; from thence along the extreme height of said mountain, to the place where Nolichucky river runs through the same; thence to the top of the Bald Mountain; thence along the extreme height of said mountain to the Painted Rock on French Broad river; thence along the highest ridge of said mountain, to the place where it is called the Great Iron or Smoky Mountain; thence along the extreme height of said mountain to the place where it is called Unicoi or Unaka Mountain, between the Indian towns of Cowee and Old Chota; thence along the main ridge of the said mountain to the southern boundary of this State, as described in the act of cession of North Carolina to the United States of America; and that all the territory, lands and waters lying west of said line, as before mentioned, and contained within the chartered limits of the State of North Carolina, are within the boundaries and limits of this State, over which the people have the right of exercising sovereignty, and the right of soil, so far as is consistent with the Constitution of the United States, recognizing the Articles of Confederation, the Bill of Rights and Constitution of North Carolina, the cession act of the said State, and the ordinance of Congress for the government of the territory north west of the Ohio; Provided, nothing herein contained shall extend to affect the claim or claims of individuals to any part of the soil which is recognized to them by the aforesaid cession act; And provided also, that the limits and jurisdiction of this State shall extend to any other land and territory now acquired, or that may hereafter be acquired, by compact or agreement with other States, or otherwise, although such land and territory are not included within the boundaries hereinbefore designated.

Section 32. That the erection of safe and comfortable prisons, the inspection of prisons, and the humane treatment of prisoners, shall be provided for.

Section 33. That slavery and involuntary servitude, except as a punishment for crime, whereof the party shall have been duly convicted, are forever prohibited in this State.

Section 34. The General Assembly shall make no law recognizing the right of property in man.

Section 35. To preserve and protect the rights of victims of crime to justice and due process, victims shall be entitled to the following basic rights:

Section 35a. The right to confer with the prosecution.

Section 35b. The right to be free from intimidation, harassment and abuse throughout the criminal justice system.

Section 35c. The right to be present at all proceedings where the defendant has the right to be present.

Section 35d. The right to be heard, when relevant, at all critical stages of the criminal justice process as defined by the General Assembly.

Section 35e. The right to be informed of all proceedings, and of the release, transfer or escape of the accused or convicted person.

Section 35f. The right to a speedy trial or disposition and a prompt and final conclusion of the case after the conviction or sentence.

Section 35g. The right to restitution from the offender.

Section 35h. The right to be informed of each of the rights established for victims.

The General Assembly has the authority to enact substantive and procedural laws to define, implement, preserve and protect the rights guaranteed to victims by this section.

Section 36. Nothing in this Constitution secures or protects a right to abortion or requires the funding of an abortion. The people retain the right through their elected state representatives and state senators to enact, amend, or repeal statutes regarding abortion, including, but not limited to, circumstances of pregnancy resulting from rape or incest or when necessary to save the life of the mother.

ARTICLE II: DISTRIBUTION OF POWERS

Section 1. The powers of the Government shall be divided into three distinct departments: the Legislative, Executive, and Judicial.

Section 2. No person or persons belonging to one of these departments shall exercise any of the powers properly belonging to either of the others, except in the cases herein directed or permitted.

LEGISLATIVE DEPARTMENT

Section 3. The legislative authority of this state shall be vested in a General Assembly, which shall consist of a Senate and House of Representatives, both dependent on the people. Representatives shall hold office for two years and senators for four years from the day of the general election, except that the speaker of the Senate and the speaker of the House of Representatives each shall hold his office as speaker for two years or until his successor is elected and qualified provided however, that in the first general election after adoption of this amendment senators elected in districts designated by even numbers shall be elected for four years and those elected in districts designated by odd numbers shall be elected for two years. In a county having more than one senatorial district, the districts shall be numbered consecutively.

Section 4. The apportionment of senators and representatives shall be substantially according to population. After each decennial census made by the Bureau of Census of the United States is available the General Assembly shall establish senatorial and representative districts. Nothing in this Section nor in this Article II shall deny to the General Assembly the right at any time to apportion one House of the General Assembly using geography, political subdivisions, substantially equal population and other criteria as factors; provided such apportionment when effective shall comply with the Constitution of the United States as then amended or authoritatively interpreted. If the Constitution of the United States shall require that legislative apportionment not based entirely on population be approved by vote of the electorate, the General Assembly shall provide for such vote in the apportionment act.

Section 5. The number of representatives shall be ninety-nine and shall be apportioned by the General Assembly among the several counties or districts as shall be provided by law. Counties having two or more representatives shall be divided into separate districts. In a district composed of two or more counties each county shall adjoin at least one other county of such district; and no county shall be divided in forming such a district.

Section 5a. Each district shall be represented by a qualified voter of that district.

Section 6. The number of senators shall be apportioned by the General Assembly among the several counties or districts substantially according to population, and shall not exceed one-third the number of representatives. Counties having two or more senators shall be divided into separate districts. In a district composed of two or more counties, each county shall adjoin at least one other county of such district; and no county shall be divided in forming such a district.

Section 6a. Each district shall be represented by a qualified voter of that district.

Section 7. The first election for Senators and Representatives shall be held on the second Tuesday in November, one thousand eight hundred and seventy; and forever thereafter, elections for members of the General Assembly shall be held once in two years, on the first Tuesday after the first Monday in November. Said elections shall terminate the same day.

Section 8. Legislative Sessions—Governor's Inauguration—The General Assembly shall meet in organizational session on the second Tuesday in January next succeeding the election of the members of the House of Representatives, at which session, if in order, the governor shall be inaugurated. The General Assembly shall remain in session for organizational purposes not longer than fifteen consecutive calendar days, during which session no legislation shall be passed on third and final consideration. Thereafter, the General Assembly shall meet on the first Tuesday next following the conclusion of the organizational session unless the General Assembly by joint resolution of both houses sets an earlier date.

The General Assembly may by joint resolution recess or adjourn until such time or times as it shall determine. It shall be convened at other times by the governor as provided in Article III, Section 9, or by the presiding officers of both Houses at the written request of two-thirds of the members of each House.

Section 9. No person shall be a Representative unless he shall be a citizen of the United States, of the age of twenty-one years, and shall have been a citizen of this State for three years, and a resident in the county he represents one year, immediately preceding the election.

Section 10. No person shall be a Senator unless he shall be a citizen of the United States, of the age of thirty years, and shall have resided three years in this State, and one year in the county or district, immediately preceding the election. No Senator or Representative shall, during the time for which he was elected, be eligible to any office or place of trust, the appointment to which is vested in the Executive or the General Assembly, except to the office of trustee of a literary institution.

Section 11. The Senate and House of Representatives, when assembled, shall each choose a speaker and its other officers; be judges of the qualifications and election of its members, and sit upon its own adjournments from day to day. Not less than two-thirds of all the members to which each house shall be entitled shall constitute a quorum to do business; but a smaller number may adjourn from day to day, and may be authorized, by law, to compel the attendance of absent members.

Section 12. Each House may determine the rules of its proceedings, punish its members for disorderly behavior, and, with the concurrence of two-thirds, expel a member, but not a second time for the same offence; and shall have all other powers necessary for a branch of the Legislature of a free State.

Section 13. Senators and Representatives shall, in all cases, except treason, felony, or breach of the peace, be privileged from arrest during the session of the General Assembly, and in going to and returning from the same; and for any speech or debate in either House, they shall not be questioned in any other place.

Section 14. Each House may punish, by imprisonment, during its session, any person not a member, who shall be guilty of disrespect to the House, by any disorderly or any contemptuous behavior in its presence.

Section 15. Vacancies. When the seat of any member of either House becomes vacant, the vacancy shall be filled as follows:

(a) When twelve months or more remain prior to the next general election for legislators, a successor shall be elected by the qualified voters of the district represented, and such successor shall serve the remainder of the original term. The election shall be held within such time as provided by law. The legislative body of the replaced legislator's county of residence at the time of his or her election may elect an interim successor to serve until the election.

(b) When less than twelve months remain prior to the next general election for legislators, a successor shall be elected by the legislative body of the replaced legislator's county of residence at the time of his or her election. The term of any Senator so elected shall expire at the next general election for legislators, at which election a successor shall be elected.

(c) Only a qualified voter of the district represented shall be eligible to succeed to the vacant seat

Section 16. Neither House shall, during its session, adjourn without the consent of the other for more than three days, nor to any other place than that in which the two Houses shall be sitting.

Section 17. Bills may originate in either House; but may be amended, altered or rejected by the other. No bill shall become a law which embraces more than one subject, that subject to be expressed in the title. All acts which repeal, revive or amend former laws, shall recite in their caption, or otherwise, the title or substance of the law repealed, revived or amended.

Section 18. Every bill shall be read once, on three different days, and be passed each time in the House where it originated, before transmission to the other. No bill shall become a law, until it shall have been read and passed, on three different days in each house, and shall have received, on its final passage in each house, the assent of a majority of all the members, to which that house shall be entitled under this constitution; and shall have been signed by the respective speakers in open session, the fact of such signing to be noted on the Journal; and shall have received the approval of the Governor, or shall have been otherwise passed under the provisions of this constitution.

Section 19. After a bill has been rejected, no bill containing the same substance shall be passed into a law during the same session.

Section 20. The style of the laws of this state shall be, "Be it enacted by the General Assembly of the State of Tennessee." No law of a general nature shall take effect until forty days after its passage unless the same or the caption thereof shall state that the public welfare requires that it should take effect sooner.

Section 21. Each House shall keep a journal of its proceedings, and publish it, except such parts as the welfare of the State may require to be kept secret; the ayes and noes shall be taken in each House upon the final passage of every bill of a general character, and bills making appropriations of public moneys; and the ayes and noes of the members on any question, shall, at the request of any five of them, be entered on the journal.

Section 22. The doors of each House and of committees of the whole shall be kept open, unless when the business shall be such as ought to be kept secret.

Section 23. Each member of the General Assembly shall receive an annual salary of $1,800.00 per year payable in equal monthly installments from the date of his election, and in addition, such other allowances for expenses in attending sessions or committee meetings as may be provided by law. The senators, when sitting as a Court of Impeachment, shall receive the same allowances for expenses as have been provided by law for the members of the General Assembly. The compensation and expenses of the members of the General Assembly may from time to time be reduced or increased by laws enacted by the General Assembly; however, no increase or decrease in the amount thereof shall take effect until the next general election for representatives to the General Assembly. Provided, further, that the first General Assembly meeting after adoption of this amendment shall be allowed to set its own expenses. However, no member shall be paid expenses, nor travel allowances for more than ninety Legislative days of a regular session, excluding the organizational session, nor for more than thirty Legislative days of any extraordinary session. This amendment shall take effect immediately upon adoption so that any member of the

General Assembly elected at a general election wherein this amendment is approved shall be entitled to the compensation set herein.

Section 24. Appropriation of public moneys. No public money shall be expended except pursuant to appropriations made by law. Expenditures for any fiscal year shall not exceed the state's revenues and reserves, including the proceeds of any debt obligation, for that year. No debt obligation, except as shall be repaid within the fiscal year of issuance, shall be authorized for the current operation of any state service or program, nor shall the proceeds of any debt obligation be expended for a purpose other than that for which it was authorized. In no year shall the rate of growth of appropriations from state tax revenues exceed the estimated rate of growth of the state's economy as determined by law. No appropriation in excess of this limitation shall be made unless the General Assembly shall, by law containing no other subject matter, set forth the dollar amount and the rate by which the limit will be exceeded. Any law requiring the expenditure of state funds shall be null and void unless, during the session in which the act receives final passage, an appropriation is made for the estimated first year's funding. No law of general application shall impose increased expenditure requirements on cities or counties unless the General Assembly shall provide that the state share in the cost. An accurate financial statement of the state's fiscal condition shall be published annually.

Section 25. No person who heretofore hath been, or may hereafter be, a collector or holder of public moneys, shall have a seat in either House of the General Assembly, or hold any other office under the state government, until such person shall have accounted for, and paid into the Treasury, all sums for which he may be accountable or liable.

Section 26. No judge of any court of law or equity, secretary of state, attorney general, register, clerk of any Court of Record, or person holding any office under the authority of the United States, shall have a seat in the General Assembly; nor shall any person in this state hold more than one lucrative office at the same time; provided, that no appointment in the Militia, or to the Office of Justice of the Peace, shall be considered a lucrative office, or operative as a disqualification to a seat in either House of the General Assembly.

Section 27. Any member of either House of the General Assembly shall have liberty to dissent from and protest against, any act or resolve which he may think injurious to the public or to any individual, and to have the reasons for his dissent entered on the journals.

Section 28. In accordance with the following provisions, all property real, personal or mixed shall be subject to taxation, but the Legislature may except such as may be held by the state, by counties, cities or towns, and used exclusively for public or corporation purposes, and such as may be held and used for purposes purely religious, charitable, scientific, literary or educational, and shall except the direct product of the soil in the hands of the producer, and his immediate vendee, and the entire amount of money deposited in an individual's personal or family checking or savings accounts. For purposes of taxation, property shall be classified into three classes, to wit: Real Property, Tangible Personal Property and Intangible Personal Property.

Real property shall be classified into four (4) sub-classifications and assessed as follows:

(a) Public Utility Property, to be assessed at fifty-five (55%) percent of its value;

(b) Industrial and Commercial Property, to be assessed at forty (40%) percent of its value;

(**c**) Residential Property, to be assessed at twenty-five (25%) percent of its value, provided that residential property containing two (2) or more rental units is hereby defined as industrial and commercial property; and

(**d**) Farm Property, to be assessed at twenty-five (25%) percent of its value. House trailers, mobile homes, and all other similar movable structures used for commercial, industrial, or residential purposes shall be assessed as real property as an improvement to the land where located.

The Legislature shall provide, in such a manner as it deems appropriate, tax relief to elderly, low-income taxpayers through payments by the state to reimburse all or part of the taxes paid by such persons on owner-occupied residential property, but such reimbursement shall not be an obligation imposed, directly or indirectly, upon counties, cities or towns. By general law, the legislature may authorize the following program of tax relief:

(**a**) The legislative body of any county or municipality may provide by resolution or ordinance that:

(**1**) Any taxpayer who is sixty-five (65) years of age or older and who owns residential property as the taxpayer's principal place of residence shall pay taxes on such property in an amount not to exceed the maximum amount of tax on such property imposed at the time the ordinance or resolution is adopted;

(**2**) Any taxpayer who reaches the age of sixty-five (65) after the time the ordinance or resolution is adopted, who owns residential property as the taxpayer's principal place of residence, shall thereafter pay taxes on such property in an amount not to exceed the maximum amount of tax on such property imposed in the tax year in which such taxpayer reaches age sixty-five (65); and

(3) Any taxpayer who is sixty-five (65) years of age or older, who purchases residential property as the taxpayer's principal place of residence after the taxpayer's sixtyfifth birthday, shall pay taxes in an amount not to exceed the maximum amount of tax imposed on such property in the tax year in which such property is purchased.

(b) Whenever the full market value of such property is increased as a result of improvements to such property after the time the ordinance or resolution is adopted, then the assessed value of such property shall be adjusted to include such increased value and the taxes shall also be increased proportionally with the value.

(c) Any taxpayer or taxpayers who own residential property as their principal place of residence whose total or combined annual income or wealth exceeds an amount to be determined by the General Assembly shall not be eligible to receive the tax relief provided in subsection (a) or (b). The Legislature may provide tax relief to home owners totally and permanently disabled, irrespective of age, as provided herein for the elderly. Tangible personal property shall be classified into three (3) sub-classifications and assessed as follows:

(a) Public Utility Property, to be assessed at fifty-five (55%) percent of its value;

(b) Industrial and Commercial Property, to be assessed at thirty (30%) percent of its value; and

(c) All other Tangible Personal Property, to be assessed at five (5%) percent of its value; provided, however, that the Legislature shall exempt seven thousand five hundred ($7,500) dollars worth of such tangible personal property which shall cover personal household goods and furnishings, wearing apparel and other such tangible property in the hands of a taxpayer. The Legislature shall have power to classify intangible personal property into sub-classifications and to establish a ratio of assessment to value in each class or subclass, and shall provide fair and equitable methods of apportionment of the value of same to this state for purposes of taxation. Banks, insurance companies, loan and investment companies, savings and loan associations, and all similar financial institutions, shall be assessed and taxed in such manner as the Legislature shall direct; provided that for the year 1973, or until such time as the Legislature may provide otherwise, the ratio of assessment to value of property presently taxed shall remain the same as provided by law for the year 1972; provided further that the taxes imposed upon such financial institutions, and paid by them, shall be in lieu of all taxes on the redeemable or cash value of all of their outstanding shares of capital stock, policies of insurance, customer savings and checking accounts, certificates of deposit, and certificates of investment, by whatever name called, including other intangible corporate property of such financial institutions. The ratio of assessment to value of property in each class or subclass shall be equal and uniform throughout the state, the value and definition of property in each class or subclass to be ascertained in such manner as the Legislature shall direct. Each respective taxing authority shall apply the same tax rate to all property within its jurisdiction. The Legislature shall have power to tax merchants, peddlers, and privileges, in such manner as they may from time to time direct, and the Legislature may levy a gross receipts tax on merchants and businesses in lieu of ad valorem taxes on the inventories of merchandise held by such merchants and businesses for sale or exchange. The portion of a merchant's capital used in the purchase of merchandise sold by him to nonresidents and sent beyond the state, shall not be taxed at a rate higher than the ad valorem tax on property. The Legislature shall have power to levy a tax upon incomes derived from stocks and bonds that are not taxed ad valorem. Notwithstanding the authority to tax privileges or any other authority set forth in this Constitution, the Legislature shall not levy, authorize or otherwise permit any state or local tax upon payroll or earned personal income or any state or local tax measured by payroll or earned personal income; however, nothing contained herein shall be construed as prohibiting any tax in effect on January 1, 2011, or adjustment of the rate of such tax. This amendment shall take effect on the first day of January, 1973.

Section 29. The General Assembly shall have power to authorize the several counties and incorporated towns in this state, to impose taxes for county and corporation purposes respectively, in such manner as shall be prescribed by law; and all property shall be taxed according to its value, upon the principles established in regard to state taxation. But the credit of no county, city or town shall be given or loaned to or in aid of any person, company, association or corporation, except upon an election to be first held by the qualified voters of such county, city or town, and the assent of three-fourths of the votes cast at said election. Nor shall any county, city or town become a stockholder with others in any company, association or corporation except upon a like election, and the assent of a like majority. But the counties of Grainger, Hawkins, Hancock, Union, Campbell, Scott, Morgan, Grundy, Sumner, Smith, Fentress, Van Buren, and the new county herein authorized to be established out of fractions of Sumner, Macon and Smith Counties, White, Putnam, Overton, Jackson, Cumberland, Anderson, Henderson, Wayne, Cocke, Coffee, Macon, Marshall, and Roane shall be excepted out of the provisions of this section so far that the assent of a majority of the qualified voters of either of said counties voting on the question shall be sufficient when the credit of such county is given or loaned to any person, association or corporation; provided, that the exception of the counties above named shall not be in force beyond the year one thousand eight hundred and eighty; and after that period they shall be subject to the three-fourths majority applicable to the other counties of the state.

Section 30. No article manufactured of the produce of this state, shall be taxed otherwise than to pay inspection fees.

Section 31. The credit of this state shall not be hereafter loaned or given to or in aid of any person, association, company, corporation or municipality; nor shall the state become the owner in whole or in part of any bank or a stockholder with others in any association, company, corporation or municipality.

Section 32. No convention or General Assembly of this state shall act upon any amendment of the Constitution of the United States proposed by Congress to the several states; unless such convention or General Assembly shall have been elected after such amendment is submitted.

Section 33. No bonds of the state shall be issued to any rail road company which at the time of its application for the same shall be in default in paying the interest upon the state bonds previously loaned to it or that shall hereafter and before such application sell or absolutely dispose of any state bonds loaned to it for less than par.

ARTICLE III: EXECUTIVE DEPARTMENT

Section 1. The supreme executive power of this state shall be vested in a governor.

Section 2. The governor shall be chosen by the electors of the members of the General Assembly, at the time and places where they shall respectively vote for the members thereof. The returns of every election for governor shall be sealed up, and transmitted to the seat of government, by the returning officers, directed to the speaker of the Senate, who shall open and publish them in the presence of a majority of the members of each House of the General Assembly. The person having the highest number of votes shall be governor; but if two or more shall be equal and highest in votes, one of them shall be chosen governor by joint vote of both Houses of the General Assembly. Contested elections for governor shall be determined by both Houses of the General Assembly, in such manner as shall be prescribed by law.

Section 3. He shall be at least thirty years of age, shall be a citizen of the United States, and shall have been a citizen of this state seven years next before his election.

Section 4. The governor shall be elected to hold office for four years and until a successor is elected and qualified. A person may be eligible to succeed in office for additional four year terms, provided that no person presently serving or elected hereafter shall be eligible for election to more than two terms consecutively, including an election to a partial term. One succeeding to the office vacated during the first eighteen calendar months of the term shall hold office until a successor is elected for the remainder of the term at the next election of members of the General Assembly and qualified pursuant to this Constitution. One succeeding to the office vacated after the first eighteen calendar months of the term shall continue to hold office for the remainder of the full term.

Section 5. He shall be commander-in-chief of the Army and Navy of this state, and of the Militia, except when they shall be called into the service of the United States. But the Militia shall not be called into service except in case of rebellion or invasion, and then only when the General Assembly shall declare, by law, that the public safety requires it.

Section 6. He shall have power to grant reprieves and pardons, after conviction, except in cases of impeachment.

Section 7. He shall, at stated times, receive a compensation for his services, which shall not be increased or diminished during the period for which he shall have been elected.

Section 8. He may require information in writing, from the officers in the executive department, upon any subject relating to the duties of their respective offices.

Section 9. He may, on extraordinary occasions, convene the General Assembly by proclamation, in which he shall state specifically the purposes for which they are to convene; but they shall enter on no legislative business except that for which they were specifically called together.

Section 10. He shall take care that the laws be faithfully executed.

Section 11. He shall, from time to time, give to the General Assembly information of the state of the government, and recommend for their consideration such measures as he shall judge expedient.

Section 12. In case of the removal of the governor from office, or of his death, or resignation, the powers and duties of the office shall devolve on the speaker of the Senate; and in case of the death, removal from office, or resignation of the speaker of the Senate, the powers and duties of the office shall devolve on the speaker of the House of Representatives.

Section 13. No member of Congress, or person holding any office under the United States, or this state, shall execute the office of governor.

Section 14. When any officer, the right of whose appointment is by this Constitution vested in the General Assembly, shall, during the recess, die, or the office, by the expiration of the term, or by other means, become vacant, the governor shall have the power to fill such vacancy by granting a temporary commission, which shall expire at the end of the next session of the Legislature.

Section 15. There shall be a seal of this state, which shall be kept by the governor, and used by him officially, and shall be called the Great Seal of the State of Tennessee.

Section 16. All grants and commissions shall be in the name and by the authority of the state of Tennessee, be sealed with the State Seal, and signed by the governor.

Section 17. A secretary of state shall be appointed by joint vote of the General Assembly, and commissioned during the term of four years; he shall keep a fair register of all the official acts and proceedings of the governor; and shall, when required lay the same, and all papers, minutes and vouchers relative thereto, before the General Assembly; and shall perform such other duties as shall be enjoined by law.

Section 18. Every bill which may pass both Houses of the General Assembly shall, before it becomes a law, be presented to the governor for his signature. If he approve, he shall sign it, and the same shall become a law; but if he refuse to sign it, he shall return it with his objections thereto, in writing, to the House in which it originated; and said House shall cause said objections to be entered at large upon its journal, and proceed to reconsider the bill. If after such reconsideration, a majority of all the members elected to that House shall agree to pass the bill, notwithstanding the objections of the executive, it shall be sent, with said objections, to the other House, by which it shall be likewise reconsidered. If approved by a majority of the whole number elected to that House, it shall become a law. The votes of both Houses shall be determined by yeas and nays, and the names of all the members voting for or against the bill shall be entered upon the journals of their respective Houses. If the governor shall fail to return any bill with his objections in writing within ten calendar days (Sundays excepted) after it shall have been presented to him, the same shall become a law without his signature. If the General Assembly by its adjournment prevents the return of any bill within said ten-day period, the bill shall become a law, unless disapproved by the governor and filed by him with his objections in writing in the office of the secretary of state within said ten-day period. Every joint resolution or order (except on question of adjournment and proposals of specific amendments to the Constitution) shall likewise be presented to the governor for his signature, and on being disapproved by him shall in like manner, be returned with his objections; and the same before it shall take effect shall be repassed by a majority of all the members elected to both houses in the manner and according to the rules prescribed in case of a bill. The governor may reduce or disapprove the sum of money appropriated by any one or more items or parts of items in any bill appropriating money, while approving other portions of the bill. The portions so approved shall become law, and the items or parts of items disapproved or reduced shall be void to the extent that they have been disapproved or reduced unless repassed as hereinafter provided. The governor, within ten calendar days (Sundays excepted) after the bill shall have been presented to him, shall report the items or parts of items disapproved or reduced with his objections in writing to the House in which the bill originated, or if the General Assembly shall have adjourned, to the office of the secretary of state. Any such items or parts of items so disapproved or reduced shall be restored to the bill in the original amount and become law if repassed by the General Assembly according to the rules and limitations prescribed for the passage of other bills over the executive veto.

ARTICLE IV: ELECTIONS

Section 1. Every person, being eighteen years of age, being a citizen of the United States, being a resident of the state for a period of time as prescribed by the General Assembly, and being duly registered in the county of residence for a period of time prior to the day of any election as prescribed by the General Assembly, shall be entitled to vote in all federal, state, and local elections held in the county or district in which such person resides. All such requirements shall be equal and uniform across the state, and there shall be no other qualification attached to the right of suffrage.

The General Assembly shall have power to enact laws requiring voters to vote in the election precincts in which they may reside, and laws to secure the freedom of elections and the purity of the ballot box.

All male citizens of this state shall be subject to the performance of military duty, as may be prescribed by law

Section 2. Laws may be passed excluding from the right of suffrage persons who may be convicted of infamous crimes.

Section 3. Electors shall, in all cases, except treason, felony, or breach of the peace, be privileged from arrest or summons, during their attendance at elections, and in going to and returning from them.

Section 4. In all elections to be made by the General Assembly, the members thereof shall vote viva voce, and their votes shall be entered on the journal. All other elections shall be by ballot.

ARTICLE V: IMPEACHMENTS

Section 1. The House of Representatives shall have the sole power of impeachment.

Section 2. All impeachments shall be tried by the Senate. When sitting for that purpose the Senators shall be upon oath or affirmation, and the Chief Justice of the Supreme Court, or if he be on trial, the Senior Associate Judge, shall preside over them. No person shall be convicted without the concurrence of two-thirds of the Senators sworn to try the officer impeached.

Section 3. The House of Representatives shall elect from their own body three members, whose duty it shall be to prosecute impeachments. No impeachment shall be tried until the Legislature shall have adjourned sine die, when the Senate shall proceed to try such impeachment.

Section 4. The Governor, Judges of the Supreme Court, Judges of the Inferior Courts, Chancellors, Attorneys for the State, Treasurer, Comptroller, and Secretary of State, shall be liable to impeachment, whenever they may, in the opinion of the House of Representatives, commit any crime in their official capacity which may require disqualification; but judgment shall only extend to removal from office, and disqualification to fill any office thereafter. The party shall, nevertheless, be liable to indictment, trial, judgment and punishment according to law. The Legislature now has, and shall continue to have, power to relieve from the penalties imposed, any person disqualified from holding office by the judgment of a Court of Impeachment.

Section 5. Justices of the Peace, and other civil officers, not hereinbefore mentioned, for crimes or misdemeanors in office, shall be liable to indictment in such courts as the Legislature may direct; and upon conviction, shall be removed from office by said court, as if found guilty on impeachment; and shall be subject to such other punishment as may be prescribed by law.

ARTICLE VI: JUDICIAL DEPARTMENT

Section 1. The judicial power of this state shall be vested in one Supreme Court and in such Circuit, Chancery and other Inferior Courts as the Legislature shall from time to time, ordain and establish; in the judges thereof, and in justices of the peace. The Legislature may also vest such jurisdiction in Corporation Courts as may be deemed necessary. Courts to be holden by justices of the peace may also be established.

Section 2. The Supreme Court shall consist of five judges, of whom not more than two shall reside in any one of the grand divisions of the state. The judges shall designate one of their own number who shall preside as chief justice. The concurrence of three of the judges shall in every case be necessary to a decision. The jurisdiction of this court shall be appellate only, under such restrictions and regulations as may from time to time be prescribed by law; but it may possess such other jurisdiction as is now conferred by law on the present Supreme Court. Said court shall be held at Knoxville, Nashville and Jackson.

Section 3. Judges of the Supreme Court or any intermediate appellate court shall be appointed for a full term or to fill a vacancy by and at the discretion of the governor; shall be confirmed by the Legislature; and thereafter, shall be elected in a retention election by the qualified voters of the state. Confirmation by default occurs if the Legislature fails to reject an appointee within sixty calendar days of either the date of appointment, if made during the annual legislative session, or the convening date of the next annual legislative session, if made out of session. The Legislature is authorized to prescribe such provisions as may be necessary to carry out Sections two and three of this article. Every judge of the Supreme Court shall be thirty-five years of age, and shall before his election, have been a resident of the state for five years. His term of service shall be eight years.

Section 4. The Judges of the Circuit and Chancery Courts, and of other Inferior Courts, shall be elected by the qualified voters of the district or circuit to which they are to be assigned. Every judge of such courts shall be thirty years of age, and shall before his election, have been a resident of the state for five years, and of the circuit or district one year. His term of service shall be eight years.

Section 5. An attorney general and reporter for the state, shall be appointed by the judges of the Supreme Court and shall hold his office for a term of eight years. An attorney for the state for any circuit or district, for which a judge having criminal jurisdiction shall be provided by law, shall be elected by the qualified voters of such circuit or district, and shall hold his office for a term of eight years, and shall have been a resident of the state five years, and of the circuit or district one year. In all cases where the attorney for any district fails or refuses to attend and prosecute according to law, the court shall have power to appoint an attorney pro tempore.

Section 6. Judges and attorneys for the state may be removed from office by a concurrent vote of both Houses of the General Assembly, each House voting separately; but two-thirds of the members to which each House may be entitled must concur in such vote. The vote shall be determined by ayes and noes, and the names of the members voting for or against the judge or attorney for the state together with the cause or causes of removal, shall be entered on the journals of each House respectively. The judge or attorney for the state, against whom the Legislature may be about to proceed, shall receive notice thereof accompanied with a copy of the causes alleged for his removal, at least ten days before the day on which either House of the General Assembly shall act thereupon.

Section 7. The judges of the Supreme or Inferior Courts, shall, at stated times, receive a compensation for their services, to be ascertained by law, which shall not be increased or diminished during the time for which they are elected. They shall not be allowed any fees or perquisites of office nor hold any other office of trust or profit under this state or the United States.

Section 8. The jurisdiction of the Circuit, Chancery and other Inferior Courts, shall be as now established by law, until changed by the Legislature.

Section 9. The judges shall not charge juries with respect to matters of fact, but may state the testimony and declare the law.

Section 10. The judges or justices of the Inferior Courts of Law and Equity, shall have power in all civil cases, to issue writs of certiorari to remove any cause or the transcript of the record thereof, from any inferior jurisdiction, into such court of law, on sufficient cause, supported by oath or affirmation.

Section 11. No judge of the Supreme or Inferior Courts shall preside on the trial of any cause in the event of which he may be interested, or where either of the parties shall be connected with him by affinity of consanguinity, within such degrees as may be prescribed by law, or in which he may have been of counsel, or in which he may have presided in any Inferior Court, except by consent of all the parties. In case all or any of the judges of the Supreme Court shall thus be disqualified from presiding on the trial of any cause or causes, the court or the judges thereof, shall certify the same to the governor of the state, and he shall forthwith specially commission the requisite number of men, of law knowledge, for the trial and determination thereof. The Legislature may by general laws make provision that special judges may be appointed, to hold any courts the judge of which shall be unable or fail to attend or sit; or to hear any cause in which the judge may be incompetent.

Section 12. All writs and other process shall run in the name of the state of Tennessee and bear test and be signed by the respective clerks. Indictments shall conclude, "against the peace and dignity of the state."

Section 13. Judges of the Supreme Court shall appoint their clerks who shall hold their offices for six years. Chancellors shall appoint their clerks and masters, who shall hold their offices for six years. Clerks of the Inferior Courts holden in the respective counties or districts, shall be elected by the qualified voters thereof for the term of four years. Any clerk may be removed from office for malfeasance, incompetency or neglect of duty, in such manner as may be prescribed by law.

Section 14. No fine shall be laid on any citizen of this state that shall exceed fifty dollars, unless it shall be assessed by a jury of his peers, who shall assess the fine at the time they find the fact, if they think the fine should be more than fifty dollars.

ARTICLE VII: STATE AND COUNTY OFFICERS

Section 1. The qualified voters of each county shall elect for terms of four years a legislative body, a county executive, a sheriff, a trustee, a register, a county clerk and an assessor of property. Their qualifications and duties shall be prescribed by the General Assembly. Any officer shall be removed from malfeasance or neglect of duty as prescribed by the General Assembly. The legislative body shall be composed of representatives from districts in the county as drawn by the county legislative body pursuant to statutes enacted by the General Assembly. Districts shall be reapportioned at least every ten years based upon the most recent federal census. The legislative body shall not exceed twenty-five members, and no more than three representatives shall be elected from a district. Any county organized under the consolidated government provisions of Article XI, Section 9, of this Constitution shall be exempt from having a county executive and a county legislative body as described in this paragraph. The General Assembly may provide alternate forms of county government including the right to charter and the manner by which a referendum may be called. The new form of government shall replace the existing form if approved by a majority of the voters in the referendum. No officeholder's current term shall be diminished by the ratification of this article.

Section 2. Vacancies in county offices shall be filled by the county legislative body, and any person so appointed shall serve until a successor is elected at the next election occurring after the vacancy is qualified.

Section 3. There shall be a treasurer or treasurers and a comptroller of the treasury appointed for the state, by the joint vote of both houses of the General Assembly who shall hold their offices for two years.

Section 4. The election of officers, and the filling of all vacancies not otherwise directed or provided by this Constitution, shall be made in such manner as the Legislature shall direct.

Section 5. Elections for judicial and other civil officers shall be held on the first Thursday in August, one thousand eight hundred and seventy, and forever thereafter on the first Thursday in August next preceding the expiration of their respective terms of service. The term of each officer so elected shall be computed from the first day of September next succeeding his election. The term of office of the governor and other executive officers shall be computed from the fifteenth of January next after the election of the governor. No appointment or election to fill a vacancy shall be made for a period extending beyond the unexpired term. Every officer shall hold his office until his successor is elected or appointed, and qualified. No special election shall be held to fill a vacancy in the office of judge or district attorney, but at the time herein fixed for the biennial election of civil officers, and such vacancy shall be filled at the next biennial election recurring more than thirty days after the vacancy occurs.

ARTICLE VIII: MILITIA

Section 1. All militia officers shall be elected by persons subject to military duty, within the bounds of their several companies, battalions, regiments, brigades and divisions, under such rules and regulations as the Legislature may from time to time direct and establish.

Section 2. The Governor shall appoint the Adjutant-General and his other staff officers; the Major-Generals, Brigadier-Generals, and commanding officers of regiments, shall respectively appoint their staff officers.

Section 3. The Legislature shall pass laws exempting citizens belonging to any sect or denomination of religion, the tenets of which are known to be opposed to the bearing of arms, from attending private and general musters.

ARTICLE IX: DISQUALIFICATIONS

Section 1. Whereas Ministers of the Gospel are by their profession, dedicated to God and the care of souls, and ought not to be diverted from the great duties of their functions; therefore, no Minister of the Gospel, or priest of any denomination whatever, shall be eligible to a seat in either House of the Legislature.

Section 2. No person who denies the being of God, or a future state of rewards and punishments, shall hold any office in the civil department of this State.

Section 3. Any person who shall, after the adoption of this Constitution, fight a duel, or knowingly be the bearer of a challenge to fight a duel, or send or accept a challenge for that purpose, or be an aider or abettor in fighting a duel, shall be deprived of the right to hold any office of honor or profit in this State, and shall be punished otherwise, in such manner as the Legislature may prescribe.

ARTICLE X: OATHS, BRIBERY
OF ELECTORS, NEW COUNTIES

Section 1. Every person who shall be chosen or appointed to any office of trust or profit under this Constitution, or any law made in pursuance thereof, shall, before entering on the duties thereof, take an oath to support the Constitution of this State, and of the United States, and an oath of office.

Section 2. Each member of the Senate and House of Representatives, shall before they proceed to business take an oath or affirmation to support the Constitution of this State, and of the United States and also the following oath: _____ do solemnly swear (or affirm) that as a member of this General Assembly, I will, in all appointments, vote without favor, affection, partiality, or prejudice; and that I will not propose or assent to any bill, vote or resolution, which shall appear to me injurious to the people, or consent to any act or thing, whatever, that shall have a tendency to lessen or abridge their rights and privileges, as declared by the Constitution of this State.

Section 3. Any elector who shall receive any gift or reward for his vote, in meat, drink, money or otherwise, shall suffer such punishment as the laws shall direct. And any person who shall directly or indirectly give, promise or bestow any such reward to be elected, shall thereby be rendered incapable, for six years, to serve in the office for which he was elected, and be subject to such further punishment as the Legislature shall direct.

Section 4. New Counties may be established by the Legislature to consist of not less than two hundred and seventy-five square miles, and which shall contain a population of seven hundred qualified voters; no line of such County shall approach the Court House of any old County from which it may be taken nearer than eleven miles, nor shall such old County be reduced to less than five hundred square miles. But the following exceptions are made to the foregoing provisions viz: New Counties may be established by the present or any succeeding Legislature out of the following Territory to wit: Out of that portion of Obion County which lies west of low water mark of Reel Foot Lake; Out of fractions of Sumner Macon and Smith Counties; but no line of such new County shall approach the Court House of Sumner or of Smith Counties nearer than ten miles, nor include any part of Macon County lying within nine and a half miles of the Court House of said County nor shall more than twenty square miles of Macon County nor any part of Sumner County lying due west of the western boundary of Macon County, be taken in the formation of said new County: Out of fractions of Grainger and Jefferson Counties but no line of such new County shall include any part of Grainger County north of the Holston River; nor shall any line thereof approach the Court House of Jefferson County nearer than eleven miles. Such new County may include any other Territory which is not excluded by any general provision of this Constitution; out of fractions of Jackson and Overton Counties but no line of such new County shall approach the Court House of Jackson or Overton Counties nearer than ten miles, nor shall such County contain less than four hundred qualified voters, nor shall the area of either of the old Counties be reduced below four hundred and fifty square miles; out of fractions of Roane, Monroe, and Blount Counties, around the town of Loudon; but no line of such new County shall ever approach the towns of Maryville, Kingston, or Madisonville nearer than eleven miles, except that on the south side of the Tennessee River, said lines may approach as near as ten miles to the Court House of Roane County. The Counties of Lewis, Cheatham, and Sequatchie, as now established by Legislative enactments are hereby declared to be Constitutional Counties. No part of Bledsoe County shall be taken to form a new County or a part thereof or be attached to any adjoining County. That portion of Marion County included within the following boundaries, beginning on the Grundy and Marion County line at the Nickajack trace and running about six hundred yards west of Ben Poseys, to where the Tennessee Coal Rail Road crosses the line, running thence south east through the Pocket near William Summers crossing the Battle Creek Gulf at the corner of Thomas Wootons field, thence running across the

Little Gizzard Gulf at Raven Point, thence in a direct line to the Bridge crossing the Big Fiery Gizzard, thence in a direct line to the mouth of Holy Water Creek, thence up said Creek to the Grundy County line, and thence with said line to the beginning; is hereby detached from Marion County, and attached to the County of Grundy. No part of a County shall be taken off to form a new County or a part thereof without the consent of two-thirds of the qualified voters in such part taken off; and where an old County is reduced for the purpose of forming a new one, the Seat of Justice in said old County shall not be removed without the concurrence of two-thirds of both branches of the Legislature, nor shall the seat of Justice of any county be removed without the concurrence of two-thirds of the qualified voters of the County. But the foregoing provision requiring a two-thirds majority of the voters of a County to remove its County seat shall not apply to the Counties of Obion and Cocke. The fractions taken from old Counties to form new Counties or taken from one County and added to another shall continue liable for their pro rata of all debts contracted by their respective Counties prior to the separation, and be entitled to their proportion of any stocks or credits belonging to such old Counties.

Section 5. The citizens who may be included in any new County shall vote with the County or Counties from which they may have been stricken off, for members of Congress, for Governor and for members of the General Assembly until the next apportionment of members to the General Assembly after the establishment of such new County.

ARTICLE XI: MISCELLANEOUS PROVISIONS

Section 1. All laws and ordinances now in force and use in this state, not inconsistent with this Constitution, shall continue in force and use until they shall expire, be altered or repealed by the Legislature; but ordinances contained in any former Constitution or schedule thereto are hereby abrogated.

Section 2. Nothing contained in this Constitution shall impair the validity of any debts or contracts, or affect any rights of property or any suits, actions, rights of action or other proceedings in Courts of Justice.

Section 3. Any amendment or amendments to this Constitution may be proposed in the Senate or House of Representatives, and if the same shall be agreed to by a majority of all the members elected to each of the two houses, such proposed amendment or amendments shall be entered on their journals with the yeas and nays thereon, and referred to the General Assembly then next to be chosen; and shall be published six months previous to the time of making such choice; and if in the General Assembly then next chosen as aforesaid, such proposed amendment or amendments shall be agreed to by two-thirds of all the members elected to each house, then it shall be the duty of the General Assembly to submit such proposed amendment or amendments to the people at the next general election in which a governor is to be chosen. And if the people shall approve and ratify such amendment or amendments by a majority of all the citizens of the state voting for governor, voting in their favor, such amendment or amendments shall become a part of this Constitution. When any amendment or amendments to the Constitution shall be proposed in pursuance of the foregoing provisions the same shall at each of said sessions be read three times on three several days in each house. The Legislature shall have the right by law to submit to the people, at any general election, the question of calling a convention to alter, reform, or abolish this Constitution, or to alter, reform or abolish any specified part or parts of it; and when, upon such submission, a majority of all the voters voting upon the proposal submitted shall approve the proposal to call a convention, the delegates to such convention shall be chosen at the next general election and the convention shall assemble for the consideration of such proposals as shall have received a favorable vote in said election, in such mode and manner as shall be prescribed. No change in, or amendment to, this Constitution proposed by such convention shall become effective, unless within the limitations of the call of the convention, and unless approved and ratified by a majority of the qualified voters voting separately on such change or amendment at an election to be held in such manner and on such date as may be fixed by the convention. No such convention shall be held oftener than once in six years.

Section 4. The Legislature shall have no power to grant divorces; but may authorize the Courts of Justice to grant them for such causes as may be specified by law; but such laws shall be general and uniform in their operation throughout the state.

Section 5. The Legislature shall have no power to authorize lotteries for any purpose, and shall pass laws to prohibit the sale of lottery tickets in this state, except that the legislature may authorize a state lottery if the net proceeds of the lottery's revenues are allocated to provide financial assistance to citizens of this state to enable such citizens to attend post-secondary educational institutions located within this state. The excess after such allocations from such net proceeds from the lottery would be appropriated to:

(1) Capital outlay projects for K-12 educational facilities; and

(2) Early learning programs and after school programs. Such appropriation of funds to support improvements and enhancements for educational programs and purposes and such net proceeds shall be used to supplement, not supplant, non-lottery educational resources for education programs and purposes. All other forms of lottery not authorized herein are expressly prohibited unless authorized by a two-thirds vote of all members elected to each house of the general assembly for an annual event operated for the benefit of a 501(c)(3) or a 501(c)(19) organization, as defined by the 2000 United States Tax Code, located in this state. A state lottery means a lottery of the type such as in operation in Georgia, Kentucky and Virginia in 2000, and the amendment to Article XI, Section 5 of the Constitution of the State of Tennessee provided for herein does not authorize games of chance associated with casinos, including, but not limited to, slot machines, roulette wheels, and the like. The state lottery authorized in this section shall be implemented and administered uniformly throughout the state in such manner as the legislature, by general law, deems appropriate.

Section 6. The Legislature shall have no power to change the names of persons, or to pass acts adopting or legitimatizing persons, but shall, by general laws, confer this power on the courts.

Section 7. The General Assembly shall define and regulate interest, and set maximum effective rates thereof. If no applicable statute is hereafter enacted, the effective rate of interest collected shall not exceed ten (10%) percent per annum. All provisions of existing statutes regulating rates of interest and other charges on loans shall remain in full force and effect until July 1, 1980, unless earlier amended or repealed.

Section 8. The Legislature shall have no power to suspend any general law for the benefit of any particular individual, nor to pass any law for the benefit of individuals inconsistent with the general laws of the land; nor to pass any law granting to any individual or individuals, rights, privileges, immunitie [immunities], or exemptions other than such as may be, by the same law extended to any member of the community, who may be able to bring himself within the provisions of such law. No corporation shall be created or its powers increased or diminished by special laws but the General Assembly shall provide by general laws for the organization of all corporations, hereafter created, which laws may, at any time, be altered or repealed, and no such alteration or repeal shall interfere with or divest rights which have become vested.

Section 9. The Legislature shall have the right to vest such powers in the Courts of Justice, with regard to private and local affairs, as may be expedient. The General Assembly shall have no power to pass a special, local or private act having the effect of removing the incumbent from any municipal or county office or abridging the term or altering the salary prior to the end of the term for which such public officer was selected, and any act of the General Assembly private or local in form or effect applicable to a particular county or municipality either in its governmental or its proprietary capacity shall be void and of no effect unless the act by its terms either requires the approval of a two-thirds vote of the local legislative body of the municipality or county, or requires approval in an election by a majority of those voting in said election in the municipality or county affected. Any municipality may by ordinance submit to its qualified voters in a general or special election the question: "Shall this municipality adopt home rule?" In the event of an affirmative vote by a majority of the qualified voters voting thereon, and until the repeal thereof by the same procedure, such municipality shall be a home rule municipality, and the General Assembly shall act with respect to such home rule municipality only by laws which are general in terms and effect. Any municipality after adopting home rule may continue to operate under its existing charter, or amend the same, or adopt and thereafter amend a new charter to provide for its governmental and proprietary powers, duties and functions, and for the form, structure, personnel and organization of its government, provided that no charter provision except with respect to compensation of municipal personnel shall be effective if inconsistent with any general act of the General Assembly and provided further that the power of taxation of such municipality shall not be enlarged or increased except by general act of the General Assembly. The General Assembly shall by general law provide the exclusive methods by which municipalities may be created, merged, consolidated and dissolved and by which municipal boundaries may be altered.

A charter or amendment may be proposed by ordinance of any home rule municipality, by a charter commission provided for by act of the General Assembly and elected by the qualified voters of a home rule municipality voting thereon or, in the absence of such act of the General Assembly, by a charter commission of seven (7) members, chosen at large not more often than once in two (2) years, in a municipal election pursuant to petition for such election signed by qualified voters of a home rule municipality not less in number than ten (10%) percent of those voting in the then most recent general municipal election. It shall be the duty of the legislative body of such municipality to publish any proposal so made and to submit the same to its qualified voters at the first general state election which shall be held at least sixty (60) days after such publication and such proposal shall become effective sixty (60) days after approval by a majority of the qualified voters voting thereon. The General Assembly shall not authorize any municipality to tax incomes, estates, or inheritances, or to impose any other tax not authorized by Sections 28 or 29 of Article II of this Constitution. Nothing herein shall be construed as invalidating the provisions of any municipal charter in existence at the time of the adoption of this amendment. The General Assembly may provide for the consolidation of any or all of the governmental and corporate functions now or hereafter vested in municipal corporations with the governmental and corporate functions now or hereafter vested in the counties in which such municipal corporations are located; provided, such consolidations shall not become effective until submitted to the qualified voters residing within the municipal corporation and in the county outside thereof, and approved by a majority of those voting within the municipal corporation and by a majority of those voting in the county outside the municipal corporation.

Section 10. A well regulated system of internal improvement is calculated to develop the resources of the state, and promote the happiness and prosperity of her citizens, therefore it ought to be encouraged by the General Assembly.

Section 11. There shall be a homestead exemption from execution in an amount of five thousand dollars or such greater amount as the General Assembly may establish. The General Assembly shall also establish personal property exemptions. The definition and application of the homestead and personal property exemptions and the manner in which they may be waived shall be as prescribed by law.

Section 12. The state of Tennessee recognizes the inherent value of education and encourages its support. The General Assembly shall provide for the maintenance, support and eligibility standards of a system of free public schools. The General Assembly may establish and support such post-secondary educational institutions, including public institutions of higher learning, as it determines. Section 13. The General Assembly shall have the power to enact laws for the protection and preservation of game and fish, within the state, and such laws may be enacted for and applied and enforced in particular counties or geographical districts, designated by the General Assembly. The citizens of this state shall have the personal right to hunt and fish, subject to reasonable regulations and restrictions prescribed by law. The recognition of this right does not abrogate any private or public property rights, nor does it limit the state's power to regulate commercial activity. Traditional manners and means may be used to take non-threatened species.

Section 14. Repealed

Section 15. No person shall in time of peace be required to perform any service to the public on any day set apart by his religion as a day of rest.

Section 16. The declaration of rights hereto prefixed is declared to be a part of the Constitution of the state, and shall never be violated on any pretense whatever. And to guard against transgression of the high powers we have delegated, we declare that everything in the bill of rights contained, is excepted out of the general powers of the government, and shall forever remain inviolate.

Section 17. No county office created by the Legislature shall be filled otherwise than by the people or the County Court. Section 18. The historical institution and legal contract solemnizing the relationship of one man and one woman shall be the only legally recognized marital contract in this state. Any policy or law or judicial interpretation, purporting to define marriage as anything other than the historical institution and legal contract between one man and one woman, is contrary to the public policy of this state and shall be void and unenforceable in Tennessee. If another state or foreign jurisdiction issues a license for persons to marry and if such marriage is prohibited in this state by the provisions of this section, then the marriage shall be void and unenforceable in this state.

SCHEDULE

Section 1. That no inconvenience may arise from a change of the Constitution, it is declared that the governor of the state, the members of the General Assembly and all officers elected at or after the general election of March one thousand eight hundred and seventy, shall hold their offices for the terms prescribed in this Constitution. Officers appointed by the courts shall be filled by appointment, to be made and to take effect during the first term of the court held by judges elected under this Constitution. All other officers shall vacate their places thirty days after the day fixed for the election of their successors under this Constitution. The secretary of state, comptroller and treasurer shall hold their offices until the first session of the present General Assembly occurring after the ratification of this Constitution and until their successors are elected and qualified. The officers then elected shall hold their offices until the fifteenth day of January one thousand eight hundred and seventy-three.

Section 2. At the first election of judges under this Constitution there shall be elected six judges of the Supreme Court, two from each grand division of the state, who shall hold their offices for the term herein prescribed. In the event any vacancy shall occur in the office of either of said judges at any time after the first day of January one thousand eight hundred seventy-three; it shall remain unfilled and the court shall from that time be constituted of five judges. While the court shall consist of six judges they may sit in two sections, and may hear and determine causes in each at the same time, but not in different grand divisions at the same time. When so sitting the concurrence of two judges shall be necessary to a decision. The attorney general and reporter for the state shall be appointed after the election and qualification of the judges of the Supreme Court herein provided for.

Section 3. Every judge and every officer of the executive department of this state, and every sheriff holding over under this Constitution, shall, within twenty days after the ratification of this Constitution is proclaimed, take an oath to support the same, and the failure of any officer to take such oath shall vacate his office.

Section 4. The time which has elapsed from the sixth day of May one thousand eight hundred and sixty-one until the first day of January one thousand eight hundred and sixty-seven shall not be computed, in any cases affected by the statutes of limitation, nor shall any writ of error be affected by such lapse of time.

John Allen,   Warren Cummings

Jesse Arledge,   Robert P. Cypert

Humphrey R. Bate,   W. V. Deaderick

Jno. Baxter,   Thomas D. Davenport

A. Blizzard,   G. G. Dibrell

Nathan Brandon,   W. F. Doherty

R. P. Brooks,   J. E. Droomgoole

James Britton,   James Fentress

Neill S. Brown,   A. T. Fielder

James S. Brown,   P. G. Fulkerson

T. M. Burkett,   Jno. A. Gardner

Jno. W. Burton,   John E. Garner

Win. Byrne,   S. P. Gaut

Alex W. Campbell,   Charles A. Gibbs

Win. Blount Carter,   B. Gordon

Z. R. Chowning,   J. B. Heiskell

James A. Coffin,   R. Henderson

H. L. W. Hill,   J. Netherland

Spl' Hill,   A. O. P. Nicholson

Sam S. House,   Geo. C. Porter

T. B. Ivie,   George E. Seay

Thomas M.,   Samuel G. Shepard

David N. Kennedy,   E. H. Shelton

D. M. Key,   Wm. H. Stephens

Sam J. Kirkpatrick,   Jno. M. Taylor

A. A. Kyle,   J. C. Thompson

Jos. A. Mabry,   W. Vance Thompson

A. G. McDougal,   James J. Turner

Malcolm McNabb,   Geo. W. Walters

Matt Martin,   Richard Warner Jr.

John H. Meeks,   Wm. H. Williamson

Thos. C. Morris,   W. M. Wright

Attest:

T. E. S. Russwurm, Secretary

Thomas W. Jones, Assistant Secretary

W. S. Kyle, 2nd Assistant Secretary

State of Tennessee

In pursuance of the fourth ordinance of the late constitutional Convention of the State of Tennessee, adopted on the Twenty-third of February One thousand eight hundred and seventy, in the City of Nashville, we D. W. C. Senter, Governor of said State, Dorsey B. Thomas, Speaker of the Senate and John C. Brown, President of said Convention, do hereby certify that we have carefully compared the votes cast for and against the New Constitution, in the election on the Fourth Saturday of March One thousand eight hundred and seventy and we certify that the vote cast in the entire State leaving out the Counties of Knox, Grainger, Roane and Overton, (from which there are no official returns) was One hundred and thirty-two thousand. Of these Ninety-eight thousand one hundred and twenty-eight votes were for the New Constitution, and Thirty-three thousand eight hundred and seventy-two votes were for the Old Constitution, and that the majority for the New Constitution is Sixty-four thousand two hundred and fifty six, and we certify accordingly the ratification of the New Constitution.

Done at the Executive Department in the City of Nashville, this fifth day of May AD One thousand eight hundred and seventy and of the American Independence the Ninety-fourth.

D. W. C. Senter, Gov

Jno. C. Brown, President

D. B. Thomas, Speaker of the Senate

www.ingramcontent.com/pod-product-compliance
Lightning Source LLC
Chambersburg PA
CBHW071242220526
45468CB00002B/968